SPIDER IN THE SKY

adapted by
ANNE ROSE

illustrated by
GAIL OWENS

Harper & Row, Publishers
New York, Hagerstown, San Francisco, London

FIRST EDITION

Library of Congress Cataloging in Publication Data
Rose, Anne K
  Spider in the sky.

  "Based upon the story 'How the Sun came' from
American Indian mythology by Alice Marriott and
Carol K. Rachlin."
  SUMMARY: Relates how Grandmother Spider brought
fire and light to the animals back in the long ago.
  1. Indians of North America—Legends.
[1. Indians of North America—Legends] I. Owens,
Gail. II. Marriott, Alice Lee, date How
the Sun came. III. Title.
E98.F6R67 1978 [398.2] [E] 76-58722
ISBN 0-06-025073-9
ISBN 0-06-025074-7 lib. bdg.

For Nana

Back in the long ago,
the animals had no heat or light.
They groped around in the dark
and shivered from cold.

"What we need is fire and light," Coyote said.
"Fire and light is what we need," Raven agreed.

A meeting was called, but it was so dim
that some of the animals lost their way
and haven't been found to this day.

When there was enough noise,
the meeting was called to order.
"There is such a thing as fire and light.
It's called the sun," Jackal said.
"It's on the other side of the mountain."

"Let's get it," cried the animals.
"Trouble is," Jackal continued,
"those who have the sun won't part with it."
"We'll take it from them," the animals yelled.
The bleating and barking were deafening.

Finally Skunk was elected to go because
he could hide the sun in his thick furry tail.

As Skunk got closer and closer to the sun,
it grew hotter and brighter,
and he had to squint away from the glare.
But he kept going.
At long last
he came to the other side of the mountain
and found the sun.

Quickly, quickly, he snapped off a piece of the sun
and hid it in his tail.
But the sun slid down his tail and escaped.

"Too bad," the animals said
when poor Skunk came back with a white streak
down the length of his bushy tail.
And still it was cold, and dark as pitch.

"Now it's my turn to go," Eagle said.
"I'll hide the sun on my head."

So Eagle flew off, traveling east as Skunk had.
Since eagles soar high, no one saw him
dive straight down out of the sky.

Swiftly, swiftly, he snatched a piece of the sun,
placed it on his head and flew off.
But the sun was so hot, it burned a hole
right through his head feathers and escaped.

"Too bad," said the animals
when poor Eagle returned with a bald head.
And still it was cold and gloomy
where the animals lived.

"A small creature could do this,"
a tiny voice said from somewhere in the grass.
Everyone spoke up at once.
"What? What? Who said that?
What was that thin voice?"

"I am Grandmother Spider," a little spider said.
"I will bring the sun's light and heat to you."

By the time the animals had stopped laughing,
Grandmother Spider was on her way.
Tied behind her web was a small pot of clay.

Spinning a silver thread as she went,
she, too, set off toward the east.
So swift and silent was she,
that no one saw her as she neared the sun.

She was so little, so very little,
and all she needed was just a tiny piece of the sun.
She reached out. Lightly, lightly,
she tweaked a piece of the sun into her pot of clay.

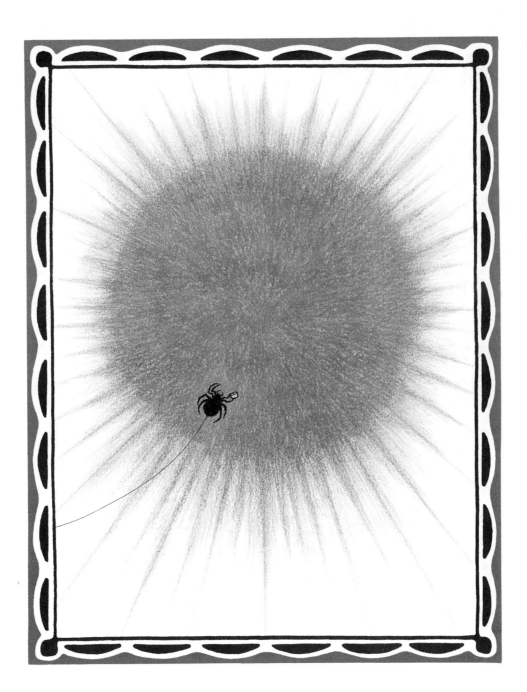

Her task done, she turned for home,
carefully following the silver thread
she herself had spun.

As she traveled,
the sun's warmth and glow shone before her
and grew wider and brighter,
as sunshine does
when it moves from east to west.

And that's how,
back in the long ago,
fire and light came to the animals.